In My Element

I AM ME!

T. Lynn Johnson

In My Element

ISBN: 978-0-578-91729-0

Butterfly Banter Publishing

DEDICATION

This little book of observational thought is dedicated to every single person in my life who has encouraged me to use my words and share what I have to say in whatever way I choose to share it.

This book is dedicated to the people who never doubted me, and simply waited on me to see what they saw, while refusing to allow me to ignore it.

TO EACH OF YOU, I LOVE YOU MORE THAN YOU WILL EVER KNOW!

In My Element

INTRODUCTION

I know I am fortunate to have come up in a time where the wisdom of elders still meant something; a time where there was a clear distinction between the adults and the children. But even with all the reverence for and to our elders, I have to be honest in saying there were instances where I did not immediately take heed their words. We had hard heads, well at least I did when it came to life lessons. And you know what they say, a hard head will make a soft…behind.

Even though we may not have listened to all the words that came from the mouths of those people we respectfully looked at as 'old folk', somehow the words they spoke always manage to penetrate our minds in such a way that it could be resurrected when we needed them in the blink of an eye. The funny part is that we are not even aware of just how much access we have to the very nectar of their existence until we reached personal points of self-discovery and discovery of real world.

We tend to romanticize the realities of the world without paying attention to the intertwining factors that weave the fabric for the life that we create for ourselves. Is life good? Of course it is; but we never fully comprehend just how good it truly is until we understand how to navigate those things that are beyond our understanding.

As I continue to grow and know, I realize that the things said to me by my mother, my father, my grandmother, my aunts, friends, and some very special spiritual angels have all served as a guide to ensure that I was able to navigate the calm and chaos of the waters I would encounter along my own personal journey. But even with the nuggets that were shared, I still did not always listen. My mama used to always say "a heap see and a few know", which is really just another way of saying, "just live baby", because one way or the other, you gon' learn.

Some of these lessons I have learned and shared with you will perhaps convey the same sentiment in different ways, and some will touch you in a place that is all too familiar. I have come to realize you can hear the same thing repeatedly for years, but until you are ready to receive it, the words will simply just float through your atmosphere of exploration until you are ready to access your place of understanding. And when you hear it, and understand it, the words are never the same, but the lessons are. Let's just say that we learn them in our own words, in our own time.

We have all experienced some thangs, and if we are honest, our needle might have been stuck on repeat (more than once) until we got tired of hearing the same scratch in our record, over and over again. Look, I broke the needle on my record and remained stuck, until I decided I needed to hear something different.

In my element (and by that I am really referring to who I am in this life at any given moment), I am Me. Sometimes, there are sprinkles on top, sometimes there are thorns. We all go through seasons, and even though some of these seasons appear to be extended stay, eventually an evolution occurs, and we become an even better version of ourselves, while discovering those little elements that make us who we truly are.

There is a dichotomy that exists in each one of us by virtue of being human; but add being a human woman to the mix, and that dichotomy becomes a magnificent miracle or a mystical mess, and the very elements that make us as calm as an ocean at sunset, can make us a torrential storm...scratch the storm, let's say a category 5 Hurricane! I chuckled at the imagery as I wrote that, because maybe just maybe, I understand the strength of the wind and water combination all too well. And if that combination grows enough strength, that wind and water will kick up the earth and start a fire. Rises and falls will always exist, but the things that help us to navigate the tide are the lessons we learn along the way.

I express my thoughts in words that illustrate the lesson, words that interpret the experience, or experiences that have given me perspective; either way, I get it eventually. Who cares how many decades it took, right?

As you read some of the lessons I have learned, even if you cannot relate, I hope there is at least one sentiment you can understand. Just know that the discovery of self and the world around us never ends, and life just keeps on happening whether we listen to what it teaches us or not.

My Observations

In My Element

I like to call myself an extroverted introvert. I am extremely introverted, with extroverted tendencies. I respect people, but I only like to be around a few, and even that has a rather quick expiration. I will always show up for my friends, but I take absolute comfort in the fact that I love my own company, even though it paves the way for over thinking; let's not even talk about that part.

Am I quiet always? Of course not. But I turn up around those who know me best, and I am very vocal when it comes to defending others. Wait, is "turn up" still the appropriate terminology. If it is or isn't, I am all of those things when I am in a space to be that. In my element, I am a quiet observer who takes in everything I see or hear. Some people cannot read me in my solitude, and that is fine with me. I will always provide a transcript if need be. One of my former bosses used to always say, "when I look at you, I just know that still waters run deep". She was not my favorite person, and all I used to think when she said it was, "you have no idea…I see you". Lol

There is power in observation. It leads to many aha moments, thoughts to ponder, and points of reflection; and that's how I gleaned many of the lessons I have learned and continue to learn. I watch, I listen, and I observe.

1

For as long as I could remember, My Granny used to say, *"It's More than a talk"*. As a kid, I always wondered what she was talking about, but as an adult, the wisdom of this short phrase always echoes loudly, and it is in that echo that I finally heard the message.

Watch what people do when their backs are against the wall, watch what people do when you don't do what they want you to do, watch what people do when your thoughts do not match theirs, watch how people respond when they cannot shake you. Just watch!

Look below the surface. People can say a lot of things; but look at what they show you. Even further, just watch because there is always more. In the famous words of Frances Shannon,

"It's more than a talk!"

2

Sometimes we spend days, months, or years fighting for the very thing we should surrender to; life is too short!

You think long, you think wrong, and before you know it the opportunity is gone. Live life and stop simply passing time.

Life is about chances, and eventually you have to take at least one.

3

Time is a terrible thing to waste. Do not waste mine and I will not waste yours. While some choose to sit still, time continues to pass and life continues to happen.

Find what makes you happy and jump in! Today is a great day to do it right!

4

As I get older, I prefer to laugh more than I cry, and smile more than I frown.
If I can bring a smile to someone else's face, I will do so gladly.
In the words of India Arie, "there's hope, it doesn't cost a thing to smile, you don't have to pay to laugh, you better thank God for that!"
Look at what is going on around us. Be thankful you're able to laugh or smile when so many others can't stop the tears from falling.

The message is clear, and life is too short to live it unhappy.

5

We cannot always have what we want, but sometimes we really do get what we expect.

Be careful, the wall you build as a defense will be the same wall that takes away the possibility of getting to know someone new; whether it is getting to know yourself, a new love, or a great new friend.

Try not to get in your own way. The only person who will lose out is you. We all deserve more. If you are going to expect anything; expect joy, not pain.

6

Things may not be where we want them to be,
but it is not as bad as it could be, and we are
far better off than we used to be.
Walk like you know what He has done for
you.
Walking against His goodness is counter-
productive, and the result is stagnation.

7

When given a choice, choose one who puts a smile on your face and joy in your heart, not one who will put a frown on your lips and cause pain from the start…

Choose to be happy, choose YOU!

8

If someone is not adding to your life, chances
are they are taking away from it. Do not
worry about offending them when you say
"ba-bye"!
Your life is a gift that you just do not just give
way. You are a blessed blessing, so keep
moving and live it like you know it!

9

Love is not all about what you are expecting
to get, it is more about what you are expected
to give—either way, it should be everything.

10

If someone or something is not adding to
your life; press delete.
If they are not contributing to your life in a
positive and productive manner, get on your
knees and let Him help you to be better.

11

Ever had one of those days when you just felt
really good? You were confident before, but
on this day; it was more than usual!
So you start to wonder why; then you
remember that you talked with God this
morning and you suddenly realize the reason!
So you smile a little brighter, and step a little
harder because you don't just have love all
over you, you have His love all over you!
What a feeling…That's God!

12

People express themselves the best way they can, whether it is with hesitation in their voice, rambling through their words, arguing to the point of lashing out, being overly nice, being uncharacteristically quiet, being excessively talkative, smiling even when sad, or laughing with tears in their eyes.

Sometimes we have to take a moment and listen to what's not being said between friends, or even acquaintances. We just might discover that we are able to heal a bruised heart, lift a shattered spirit, nourish a soul, or even realize that our outstretched hand has captured a heart that mirrors the beat of our own, if only we would just listen.

Life is full of surprises, step outside of yourself and you just might find a beautifully wrapped blessing.

13

People say you should not burn bridges, but let's be honest; there are some bridges that need to be set ablaze! Just make sure you do not try to go backwards to cross it again, because chances are, you will drown.

Just light it up and keep moving!

14

If you continue to walk around with blinders on (by choice), the brick wall you run into will surely open your eyes. Unfortunately, it will be too late, and you will not be able to avoid the bruises.

15

If you know you want more, then settling for less should not be an option.

16

Even though we know the tremendous power
of words, it is still amazing how the stanza of
a poem, or the lyrics of a song can transport
you back to a memory, meet you at your
current reality, or give you a glimpse into what
could be. Good, bad, or ugly, words have
IMPACT!

17

Welcome each morning with at least a piece
of a smile, even if it feels like the 3rd Monday
of the week!
Gotta love it!

18

If you are traveling in my direction, come aboard. If not, the ocean is very large, feel free to set your own sail.

19

Do not allow the fantasy you create in your mind to confuse the reality of any situation. That is called wasting time and life is much too short for that.

Live without dwelling!

20

Regardless of what you do, a great mother always sees more in you than you see in yourself. She knows when to hold you, and when to let you go. She knows when to go at you easy, but you better believe she knows when to go at you hard!
A mother will pick you up when you fall and at the same time encourage you when you need to do the heavy lifting and pick yourself up.
No matter what you go through there is no love like hers.

21

Never make apologies for who you are. Perfection is unattainable for the common man, but surely we can all be better. Be honest about the changes you need to make and make them for you, not to please the masses.

Some will come along for the journey, so stretch your hands out to receive them; but there are some you will lose along the way, and that is fine. Quite honestly, some excess baggage is not worth the additional fare.

22

We often hold back what we really want to say for fear that it will hurt others, push them further away, or make them angry; when the truth is, sometimes the very thing we hold back is not only the release we need to go forward, it is also the lesson someone else may need to be taught.

All lessons are not pleasant. Have enough courage to teach it anyway, in hopes that others will be open enough to learn it, and in a place to receive it.

Simply put, sometimes holding your tongue is the right thing to do, at other times, it can be a hindrance.

Allow common sense to direct this choice.

23

When you give the benefit of the doubt, it can also mean issuing yourself an invitation to disappointment.

24

Embracing anger means you will flirt with bitterness. Flirting with bitterness means you will court resentment. These encounters keep you from basking in His glory, mingling with true happiness, and having a lifelong love affair with complete joy.

Letting go of pain, hurt, or anger isn't an easy process, but knowing that somehow the blessings that God has for you (not those you have for yourself) is on the other side your ability to truly let go makes it a little easier.

It may sound strange but you sometimes you have to release to receive.

25

Let the venom of a snake be the fuel that
boosts your momentum.

26

Settling is knowing you are more than enough and still accepting less than you deserve. If you do not recognize your worth, no one else will.

Figure it out.

27

I am thankful for the things that have happened (past), the things that are happening (present), and all of the things to come (future), and without a doubt, I am thankful to a God merciful enough to bring me through each and every experience with the love of great family and friends.

28

In honest reflection, we will realize that all things we tried to do in our strength resulted in hurt, pain, or frustration. It is not until we loosen our grips on the reigns of life that He can step in and take control. We deserve far more than we settle for in work, in love, and in life. We are our only deterrent to having all the joy we can stand. So live life on purpose and trust the man upstairs to handle the rest. There must be preparation before designation.

Simply Put: You cannot have it if you're not ready for it.
Get ready, Get ready!

29

A wolf in sheep's clothing is still a wolf. Just watch, pay attention, and listen. The arrogance they possess will not allow them to resist howling at the moon.

30

When we find the strength to let go of the people, things and circumstances that weigh us down, it is then that we develop the courage to use those same hands to embrace and hold on to those that lift us up. We all have the ability to create new circumstances.

Let the creating begin!

31

Experiences breed memories. Some will make you smile and burst into laughter, while others will bring tears to your eyes and force you to visit places of pain, brokenness, or sorrow. Sometimes we want to remember the good and ignore the bad; or dwell on the bad and disregard the good. Each has shaped us into the person we are becoming and therefore they should be remembered accordingly.

Hold on to your experiences. The good ones remind you of what could be, and the bad ones remind you about what you should not repeat. Each is important.

32

Life is full of lessons. When you begin to ascend to higher levels (in life, love, careers-whatever it is you seek), stumbling blocks of varying natures emerge in the form of people or circumstances. Sometimes it's a sneak tactic, sometimes it's a full-fledged ambush. But fear not, if you are walking the path that has been set for you, these blocks won't be able to deter you. Just clear your pathway of unwanted debris and keep trucking.

When it comes to stumbling blocks, know which ones to go around and which ones to step on.

33

We often want these perfect conditions before we move. We want a guarantee of the end before we make a step toward the beginning; all the while failing to understand that it's the journey in between that's important. If it is a God-led journey, remove all doubt and trust that He will accompany you along the way. The conditions for movement may never be perfect, but the Truly Perfect One has already paved the path toward your destiny. He's just waiting on you to move toward it.

Move when you're led to move. Resist stagnation in every facet of your life. What good is the dream if you are not willing to chase it.

34

People perpetrate a FRAUD, FAKE the funk, and put on a FAÇADE, ultimately earning an "F" for falsifying facts in this life. You were automatically born grade "A" because you were authentically created by an ALL-KNOWING AUTHOR. If you must wear a mask to please people, give them a wave for Bye-Bye!

Don't be so quick to put on a show. Fiction is entertaining, but eventually the curtain closes and the stage goes black. Just be you, there is no one better.

35

Sometimes there's no explanation or reason, it just is. Some things aren't meant to be figured out, so don't try. Sometimes feelings hit you that you're not prepared for; deal with them. Sometimes you have a gut feeling about things and people that you alone have no definitive answer for; that feeling is not by chance. If you are connected to the Master, it's not just a gut feeling; it's discernment. He has the answers, and if you are connected, chances are that you already know them too.

Have a little faith. You do not have to have all of the answers, just trust that He does.

36

The concept of "more" is all relative; but one thing's for sure, you don't get more if you don't give more.

We can't expect more of anything if we are not willing to give our everything.

37

Some days are better than others, but every day is a gift. We must choose whether or not we open the package or discard it. Opening it reveals the dawn of a new day, while discarding it leaves us stuck in yesterday's darkness.

No matter how many tears you've cried or how many trials you've gone through, never be afraid to try something new.

38

If you have to convince 'em, don't join 'em, and if they have to convince you, just RUN!

Forced fits look good for a second, but eventually the pain is hell on your feet. Don't waste your time on things and people that don't deserve it. You will know the perfect fit when you feel it.

39

Life is a journey that most don't want to travel alone. If you desire to have company along the way, realize that forward movement is the only choice. We can move forward together, but self-imposed stagnation is a solo mission. Choose to move out of your comfort zone and find the desire to grow.

The past is a footstool, not an anchor. Rise above it, don't let it weigh you down.

40

If the sound of your voice can bring a smile to another's face, keep letting your voice be heard by them.

That makes you kind of special

41

Words make love to your ears, but when the action matches the word; that's when love is being made to your heart.

42

Know who you are and whose you are. You never have to convince anyone that they're missing out on you. Once they realize what they have lost, it won't require any explanations. Time is forward moving. It waits on no one.

43

Never try to compete with a past someone has allowed to take up residence in their present. Instead, allow your presence to be embraced by 'the one' who sees you as a gift in their life today, knowing they couldn't imagine their life without you tomorrow.

Always remember that you are the grand prize, not the parting gift.

44

As you mature, there's a shift in what matters most. You care less about what others think & more about what's best for you; your desire to please others shifts to a desire to please The Man Upstairs. Selfish ways transform into selfless actions, temporary wants fail to satisfy as permanent needs rightfully take precedence and external gratification gives way to internal peace.

The full-length movie is far better than the trailer IF you allow The Director, The Writer & The Producer to do the job.

Little things matter most, the rest is just a bonus.

45

Sometimes ya gotta chuckle so ya don't buckle.

46

We can spend so much time living for others, that we don't know how to handle that same life when we start living for ourselves.

Stop the madness!

47

People show you what they want their world to see. Don't get caught up in the entertainment; embrace your own reality show.

You've been blessed with a life of your own, as my granny and my mama would say, "you just live baby"

48

You won't always understand why the road you stumbled upon has been paved with so many curves, bumps, & craters. All you really need to know is that the right navigation will get you to the other side.

Incomprehensible doesn't mean impassable. Just keep on trucking.

All in due time child, all in due time!

49

Be sure that your flame fanners don't double
as flame snuffers.

Life is full of lessons, learn from each.

50

Be thankful for the good & the bad. It builds and strengthens your character & it also makes you resilient.

Wisdom says, "you can make it through anything as long as you keep moving; have an attitude of gratitude as you trudge along"

51

Hidden agendas have predetermined benefactors and it's usually not you. You have to have your own best interest at heart to recognize when others do or don't.

52

You have to have a heart with a pathway to forgiveness and sometimes a road to redemption. At some, point we have all done wrong, fallen short & required forgiveness and/or redemption. Who are we to look down on another for trying to fix their wrongs? Their sin is no greater or less than yours.

Wisdom says, "sweep around your own doorstep before u condemn someone else's house".

53

Whether you're at your highest or lowest, the people who love you will love you at any level & try to lift you or push you in the direction that's best for you.

Wisdom says, everyone who says they are there for you, really aren't; all help ain't good help & difficult times reveal true people.

54

Step out of your box. Do the thing you think
you cannot do. Don't be afraid to do things
you've never done & have the courage to
experience things you never thought you
would; you just might like it.

Laugh until you cry! There's joy in the
journey & peace in the release. You can't do
anything wearing a cape of fear,

Wisdom says, accept a challenge, embrace
change.

55

If it were not for the struggle, we wouldn't understand the progress; if it weren't for the mistakes, the lessons would be impenetrable; if it were not for the hurt, the joy would be inconceivable. If it were not for a little bit of faith, we'd always be led by a whole lotta fear.

Perfection does not equate to peace, but there's peace in knowing that there's purpose in the broken pieces.

56

You might not always know where you're going, but knowing where you don't want to be is a good start to getting there.

57

When you sell yourself short, do not be surprised when other people capitalize on the discount.

Trust Yourself!

58

You can continue to replay the same record over & over, but the thing is, the lyrics won't change, and the record will eventually scratch. You have to move your hands from the repeat button in order to advance to another track.

You can only move forward if you're going in that direction.

59

In the areas of life that require constant growth, comfort can often breed complacency. Every now & then, you have to wiggle a bit.

Comfort is necessary for shoes, but even with those, you may have to experience a bit of discomfort to pull off the impact you want to have.

It's great to make strides, but sometimes you have to set out to conquer the waves.

60

I am the best of who I am wherever I am
regardless of when I am there.

61

You do not always need to surround yourself
with an "amen" corner; sometimes you need a
dose of reality from the "what the hell"
section.

62

It's not always the restraints that others place on you that hold you back, sometimes it's the limitations you place on yourself.

63

There is sometimes a break before the breakthrough.

Greater is coming!

64

The thing about going nowhere is that it really doesn't take that long to get there. Traveling aimlessly keeps you right where you are. Move with intention, not apprehension.

Pursue your promise!

65

You cannot be anything to anyone until you
are everything to yourself.

Know your worth!

66

Laugh lines, frown lines, or you don't even wanna know lines; they are yours! It is up to you to decide which ones you use more.

67

Sometimes we get so busy seeking praise that we neglect the promise & disregard the purpose.

68

The next level is always attainable, but it seems just a little closer when you have access to someone who took the stairs before you.

Use your tools!

Live and Learn!

69

If more is what you want, complacency is a common place in which you should refuse to dwell; be mindful of those who encourage you to renew the lease.

70

You know those friends that tell you what you don't want to hear, when you don't want to hear it; the ones that save you from yourself; the ones you ignore for an hour or a day or a week or so because you know they were right and you just didn't wanna say so right then...the ones who will wipe your tears, make u cry, and laugh at you all at the same dang time...they are all of that and so much more! What would you ever do without them?!?

71

There are some things in life you will never understand. Resolve to stop trying to figure it all out. Whatever you are supposed to know, rest assured, He will show you; just be sure you're prepared for the revelation.

72

When loyalty becomes a liability eventually it results in a casualty. Do the right things for the right reason.

73

You will never pass some of life's repeated tests until you commit to not cheating yourself. A learned lesson can unlock a blessin'.

74

Sometimes we're conditioned to freak out at every distraction, and every hurdle.

It's not what you encounter, it's how you encounter the encounter!

75

As sure as you live & breathe, you will be tested (probably more than you would like). Even when it's hardest, you have to remember that the Creator of the test is far more important than the administrator of the test...It won't always be easy, but He knows what you need and what to use to get you there.

Breathe & keep it moving!

76

Sometimes you struggle where you are to harness the strength & courage to go where you are supposed to be.

Listen when you are led!

77

We all have our own 'lot' in life. Not everyone, everything, or every issue deserves a parking space.

Who or what you allow to take up space in your life can change the entire landscape.

Do not be afraid to say:

RESERVED PARKING ONLY, TOWING STRONGLY ENFORCED!

78

What you feed will grow, but also know that
what you neglect will show.

79

A lesson for the young, the not so young, and those old enough to know better:

In anything, second-hand information leads to first class confusion & chaos. Find out for yourself. Go to the source, especially when you're getting outsourced information.

Word to the Wise: when you jump on the wrong bandwagon, don't be surprised when those are the very wheels that run you over.

80

Intelligence cannot be purchased, and an absence of true knowledge is always evident. It's all of that power in the tongue that we often underestimate. What you say can harm others, but let's not forget that what you say can also eliminate you.

listening is more than just hearing

81

You cannot morph into someone else's idea of who you are or how you should be simply for attention, personal gain, appearances, etc. Going along to get along does guarantee a step in some direction, it just may not be the direction you're supposed to go.

Conformity doesn't always lead to comfort. Why fit into someone else's mold when you have the capacity to create your own!

82

Don't cheapen yourself in search of anyone else's validation (personally or professionally). Don't allow a price tag to be placed on something so priceless...YOU!

83

Never put yourself in a position to regret the
chances you didn't take.

84

Fear can be a faith stealer and a joy
blocker...release your fears, all of them!

85

No one can tell you who you are if you already know. Be true to yourself.

86

You have to keep on keeping on even if it
means removing yourself from an association
or a situation; and do it without apology.
Sometimes you just have to honestly say,
"Don't take my distance as an insult, think of
it as a safety precaution."

87

True change is made by choice, and if you did not make the choice, chances are the change will not stick. If you are not "real" to the reflection in the mirror, you become a fraud to yourself.

88

Don't take up residence in a box u were never meant to stay in...as a matter of fact, forget the box.

89

The good thing about broken pieces is that you can put those bad boys back together stronger than they were before. Your "I've been through phase" sets the stage for your "I made it through" declaration. We all have a story & we control our own narrative...

It's not about what's thrown at you, it's how you orchestrate the play.

90

If you do the same, expect the same, and remain the same...what changes? NOTHING.

Sometimes you have to step outside of your normal so you can reach your optimal.

91

Sometimes all you need is......SILENCE.

Moments of solitude can work wonders for your attitude.

92

Everything that matches does not necessarily go together. Don't modify who you are to meet someone else's need. The truth of who you are will always reveal itself, so be unapologetically you and allow the right people to make the discovery.

93

You cannot win if you are hell bent on starting from a place of self-defeat. You are responsible for what you think.

94

There is a difference between a display of
genuine passion, and a feeble attempt at
posturing; it's not hard to tell, ask a child.
They can spot a fake a mile away.

95

If you continue to discount your worth, don't be surprised when people take you at face value.

96

Sometimes you have to come face to face with your demons in order to slay them. You can't conquer what you refuse to face.

97

People attempt to insult your intelligence because they ASSume you are blind to the realities of their mess. Sometimes, tunnel vision can distort your peripheral; see what is in front of you, but also pay attention to the details.

98

Your been through can pave the way for someone else's get through. Do not hesitate to help pull someone else out of a hole just because you were able to climb out of it.

99

We prune trees for the same reasons that we cut dead ends from our hair: to promote growth. The problem is, so many of us don't realize that dead ends exist in more places in their lives than just their hair.

The only way to make room for growth is to remove the things that are taking up space.

100

It is a blessing to know that the people in your corner cheer louder for you than you could ever cheer for yourself at times. They are your 'amen corner', the 'what the hell' hollerers, the 'are you crazy' collective and the 'I know you can' crew.

Be thankful for your pushers and your praisers, they are priceless!

101

The limited base of knowledge when it comes to people of color, no matter where we live or where we came from is startling, but not surprising. You cannot guide, lead, or teach those you have no true interest in acquiring knowledge about. I don't care what race you are or what your political affiliation might be. If you're in politics, education, or any other field, you have to care about the people you impact, in order to make an impact.

102

People are relying on your ignorance, your
absence, and your fear. You cannot
REshackle the boundless.

103

The perfect COMPLEMENT is far more
beneficial than the perfect COMPLIMENT.

104

Many of our choices impact the masses,
which means that sometimes we have to think
beyond our own prejudices and agendas. In
the blink of an eye, we can so easily move
from TREASURE to TRAVESTY just
because we failed to count up the costs. Just
look at the world around us.

It is impossible to retract a bullet once you've
pulled the trigger.

Choices have consequences.

105

They say you are what you eat, but you are also the company you keep.

Surround yourself with people who encourage your growth, not those who stunt it.

Pocket change adds up, there's no value in lint!

106

Too often we echo ignorance and totally disregard the impact that it has on those who cannot even speak for themselves...thus the voiceless become the casualties of people making a whole lot of noise.

107

We get so caught up in words without any focus on action. Remember: Every open book isn't non-fiction. Some stories are for entertainment purposes only.

108

Narrowed perspectives can often lead to missed opportunities; sometimes the only place tunnel vision leaves you is in a dang tunnel!

109

Be more faithful to the reflection in the mirror than you are to the court of public opinion. You cannot do you if you're sitting there waiting on someone else to tell you who you are.

110

You will always be an expert at one thing no one could ever dictate to you...being yourself. Embrace the beauty, the mess, the joy, the fight, the clumsiness, the steadiness, the softness, the hardness, the genius, and the dork! Embrace everything that makes you who you are, because you are worth more than anything.

Your life is meant to be lived not leveraged.

111

You don't have to hear a person say where he stands when you can clearly see their stance.

112

One can't disavow what they've encouraged in the first place…that would only prove that they're a liar; a fact that everyone would likely know anyway, even if they try to pretend that they don't know.

113

When people talk a lot without saying anything more often than not it's because (1) they don't know anything or (2) they're afraid that you know too much.

114

Scripted empathy does not translate into a compassionate soul; a fragile ego accompanied by a spineless frame will always revert to type.

115

Standing behind the ways of a fool doesn't make you smart, it makes you an accessory.

116

True colors may stay suppressed for a while,
but they never stay hidden.

117

The release restores the freedom you stole
from yourself.

118

Being stuck on figuring out the why won't necessarily lead you to the know; but trusting the WHO will get you through to the other side.

119

You cannot avoid the test and expect to
master the lesson.

120

It's hard to comprehend the perceptions of others when you can't find a way to see beyond the confines of self. Change comes about through acceptance; acceptance is often the byproduct of awareness. You can't ignore reality and expect magic to take care of it

121

Transformation requires an unveiling, a stripping down of ill-fitting material to be replaced by tailored garments; the exposing of darkness to pave way for light, the acknowledgement of complacency to garner the courage to leverage upward mobility. It requires malleability, not conformity & admission not avoidance. Transformation requires access to your truth & it's your story to tell.

122

Compassion & empathy are essential to those who practice them and fodder to those who prey on them. Never change the heart that you have to care about others; just know that sometimes you will have to channel a spirit that discerns & a mind that can see further than you feel. In other words, sift through the bull and guard your hearing because if you're not careful, you'll internalize the fallacies of someone else's contrived truths simply because you cared enough to lend an ear.

There's a difference between being a sounding board and being a dumping ground. Don't allow friends, family, lovers, co-workers, or anyone else to pour their acid into your soul just so that they can have an amen corner while you carry all of the bricks they created.

It's ok to silence the sender.

123

When I was younger, I used to smile with my mouth closed, but was always told that I had a pretty smile even though I never showed my teeth. I can remember smiling for pictures when I was younger & never showing my them because I did not like them very much at the time. Then when I got older, I got myself some braces, straightened it all out and my pretty smile then became beautiful to me.

My point is not to express that my single dimpled smile has become one of my greatest assets, in my opinion. My point is that if I had settled on someone else's version of pretty, I would have never aimed for and captured my own version of beautiful and this has little to do with my smile.

Change comes to us or through us & the way we choose to navigate the current determines whether our lives will reflect someone's version of Ok or our own version of great.

In My Element

Our version does not mean someone else's version is wrong; it just means it is different from ours.

~Sometimes it takes a while to see in yourself what others see in you~

124

We can spend a lifetime doing something we've learned to be good at without ever scratching the surface of the exhilaration felt when you're doing something you absolutely love.

A gift is useless if left unopened and pointless if left unused. It cannot make a way if you don't get out of the way. You gotta make a move in order to improve.

Passion+Purpose=Pathway to Progression

You have to be present to discover the gift.

125

When a person is quiet or still, some take it to mean docile, weak, unaware, disinterested… They immediately default to the negatives that can result from silence, without taking a second to realize the positives. Sometimes, that misunderstood silence is a superior example of strength, restraint and drive. I can tell you with certainty that on the strength of my silence & stillness alone, lives have been metaphorically saved from words that could cut so deeply that resuscitation would be required for recovery.

Observation, strategy, reflection…they all often occur in silence. As soon as silence becomes intimidating or uncomfortable, the next thing is "I can't read them, they don't say much." If the person wants to be read by you, they would provide you with a transcript. It is during these times that instead of questioning someone else's silence, use your own to observe & pay attention.

In My Element

Words aren't the only way to communicate. There's power in observation & all silence is not void of sound. Impactful action is often preceded by necessary silence & stillness. You don't have to do a lot of talking to be understood and talking endlessly doesn't mean you've said a thing!

Silence is never really quiet.

126

Sometimes we get so caught up in what it sounds like that we pay no attention to what it is. All help isn't good help, all money isn't good money, and every handout isn't meant to lift you up.

People count on you to be so impressed with decorated mess that you forget to look beneath the surface at all the stipulations they attempt to suppress.

(I didn't mean to rhyme at the end but oh well...pay attention). Don't be swooned by swine

Don't just scratch the surface, dig beneath it.

127

It can be attributed to culture, or even personal choice, but even from a child I knew not to eat from everyone, no matter whose "table" it was. If I don't perceive you to be clean, I won't eat from you; if I don't trust you, I won't eat from you; if you don't like me, I won't eat from you and if I don't like you, I'd feed you ONLY from the kindness of my heart. My point is, you can't be so quick to swallow manure just because it doesn't look like $#&@. You can still smell it, even if the look of it has been masked. 'A seat at the table' doesn't always grant you access, sometimes it just makes you a convenient accessory.

Dialogue is vital & communication is necessary, but do not confuse momentary pacification with sustained elevation.

There's no need to read between the lines when it's all written in plain sight.

You cannot eat from every table that offers you a seat; pack a snack.

128

One day, as I sat in the backseat (with my niece driving), I was reminded of how incredibly hard it is for so many to step aside and relinquish control (even if they were the teacher). At any given moment, a leader needs to know how to stand up, but they also need to know when to stand down. When you have an inability to step back, you may present yourself as controlling, micromanaging, or something else altogether.

The thing is, when you operate in that manner, at some point, the only person to tolerate you is you. Find a balance. Trust your ability to lead by also demonstrating your ability to follow when it is necessary. It's never comfortable to be a passenger, especially when you're used to being the driver.

Don't just know how to play your position, know when you need to transform it.

In My Element

Metaphorically speaking, having a license to drive (and more experience to do so), doesn't always mean you're the best choice to navigate the vessel.

~Parameters do come with position;
sometimes you gotta hold your mule~

129

My mama puts up 9-foot trees, and for years I have wanted one of those trees for myself so I would always ask about it and she'd say, "don't pay full price, just wait 'til the end of the season."

Well, mama knows how to find a deal and a few years back my 9-footer was housed in her garage until I could pick it up. She got it at the end of the season, just like she said, and paid little to nothing for it. That is a lesson in strategy and patience, but that is not the lesson of this passage.

Once I had the tree, my mama jokingly said, "you know you might not be able to put that tree up by yourself." I asked her why and her response was simply, "you're too short." My only response was to prove her wrong.

We are often willing to go out of our way to prove to someone else that we can do something because they doubt us; but how often do we go out of our way to prove to ourselves that we can do something when we have doubted ourselves? The true answer is NOT OFTEN ENOUGH.

Don't always go the extra mile to prove something to someone else, start by going the extra mile (and then some) to prove something yourself.

There's no benefit in self-doubt.

130

My grandmother (Francis Shannon) used to say, "watch out for counterfeit people." Her words were a bit more colorful, but let's just go with that!

There's a lot to be said for the wisdom of our elders. In quiet reflection and observation (or even in noisy invasion), so much can be seen when we look at the world around us. When people can't deal with the elevation of you, they attempt to initiate the assassination of you...by trying to kill your character, seeking to taint your reputation, marginalizing your impact, replicating what you originated, or (in the words of this generation) just being plain petty. You have to press on anyway without thought or worry. Duplicity is always discovered.

People can pick apart greatness, but they can't erase the knowledge of it once it's been realized, no matter how hard they try.

The inability to ACKNOWLEDGE a thing, does not erase the KNOWLEDGE that it exists.

There's

ALWAYS

More......

In My Element

For as long as I can remember, I have been an observer and an over thinker. But the most important part is that while I think, I feel. Those feelings derive from moments, that came from experiences that were mine and mine alone, or from moments where I simply beared witness. Either way, they all revealed lessons that needed to be learned. The how, when, and why of the acquisition of these lessons are a topic for another time. But just let me just remind you that I had to repeat a whole lot of them before I comprehended what needed to be understood.

Before I even put all of these thoughts together, I started trying to categorize them. You know, code them for life, love, work and all that jazz; but as hard as I initially tried, I could not do it. Wait, let me be a little more truthful. I didn't really try that hard to do it because the moment I started, I realized that made zero sense to me.

I have come to learn that life happens how it happens, and it definitely doesn't go down in neat, sequentially categorized episodes, or in any type of order that we could ever fathom or plan for ourselves. Ready or not, life just comes at us and all we can do is live it anyway.

I do not think it was a mistake or a coincidence that my grandmother's words anchored the beginning and the end all of the things I have learned in the middle. I had no clue what she meant by "it's more than a talk," but I definitely know now; and as my vocabulary grew, I knew exactly what she meant by "watch out for counterfeit people". It all makes me laugh out loud often; especially when you see a physical representation of her words in your real life situations.

When you can look back on the lesson, and realize you finally mastered the test (at least one or two), it will make you chuckle a little or cry a lot when you look back on what you had to experience to finally get it!

It is my hope that you have been able to take at least one thing away from what the thoughts that I have shared, and that you also understand the necessity to explore and share your own in whatever way you choose. We do not just learn from our own experiences; we learn from the experiences of others.

At some point, we will each realize that there is a lesson in everything, and it is okay that we grasp them at different moments, in different ways and at different times knowing that we will get all of it when

we have reached our time for learning and

understanding.

We Learn by Living…

We evolve by teaching…

We understand by and by!!!

In My Element

Just
A Little
Extra...

I do not only grasp lessons during moments of observation, I also grasp them in moments of quiet reflection to be shared via my version of poetry...

TAKE A PEEK!

In My Element

In my element,
I am the sum total of my experiences
And the budding manifestation of His plan.
I am the culmination of my choices,
The totality of my expression is guided by a gentle
nudge from His hands.

In my element,
I am the calm before the storm,
And the breath you inhale for a reprieve,
I am also a categorical collective of firestorms
When witnessing wrongs meant to deceive.

In my element,
I'm a cool cup of water on a hot summer's day,
And the cool breeze that soothes your soul;
But catch me at the just the right moment
And I'm a hailstorm of protection for each PEACE
of my heart's gold.

In my element,
You can't quite detect the frequency of my waves
Or comprehend my ember scribed scripts on sight;
You might not be able sift through the sands of my
time,
Unaware that my time of solace gives a lift to my
spirit's height!

In My Element

In my element,
I have become completely unapologetic,
For each imperfection and every idiosyncrasy,
I choose to embrace the embodiment of all that I am,
Because In My Element, I AM ME!

There's More to Come!

In My Element